# CELEBRATING THE NAME ANGELA

# Celebrating the Name Angela

Walter the Educator

Silent King Books

Copyright © 2024 by Walter the Educator

All rights reserved. No part of this book may be reproduced in any manner whatsoever without written permission except in the case of brief quotations embodied in critical articles and reviews.

First Printing, 2024

Disclaimer
This book is a literary work; poems are not about specific persons, locations, situations, and/or circumstances unless mentioned in a historical context. This book is for entertainment and informational purposes only. The author and publisher offer this information without warranties expressed or implied. No matter the grounds, neither the author nor the publisher will be accountable for any losses, injuries, or other damages caused by the reader's use of this book. The use of this book acknowledges an understanding and acceptance of this disclaimer.

dedicated to everyone with the first name of Angela

# ANGELA

In lands where dreams cascade like silver streams,

# ANGELA

Angela reigns, a queen in radiant beams.

# ANGELA

Her name, a melody that fills the air,

# ANGELA

A symphony of grace beyond compare.

# ANGELA

In gardens blooming with celestial hues,

# ANGELA

Angela walks, her steps like morning dews.

# ANGELA

Each petal whispers secrets to her ear,

# ANGELA

In her presence, all sorrows disappear.

# ANGELA

From whispered winds to oceans deep and wide,

# ANGELA

Angela's name is hailed with love and pride.

# ANGELA

It dances on the lips of poets bold,

# ANGELA

In verses spun from stories yet untold.

# ANGELA

In forests where the ancient spirits dwell,

# ANGELA

Angela's name, a sacred, mystic spell.

# ANGELA

It echoes through the trees with gentle sighs,

# ANGELA

A blessing whispered 'neath the starlit skies.

# ANGELA

In realms where magic weaves its potent charm,

# ANGELA

Angela's name ignites a fiery calm.

# ANGELA

It lights the way through shadows dark and deep,

# ANGELA

A beacon of hope when weary souls weep.

# ANGELA

In cities bustling with life's endless race,

# ANGELA

Angela's name brings solace and embrace.

# ANGELA

It weaves a tapestry of joy and mirth,

# ANGELA

A testament to her enduring worth.

# ANGELA

In fields where flowers bloom with vibrant hue,

# ANGELA

Angela's name is sung by birds anew.

# ANGELA

It floats upon the breeze with soft caress,

# ANGELA

A tender kiss to banish all distress.

# ANGELA

In every heart where love and longing dwell,

# ANGELA

Angela's name casts its enchanting spell.

# ANGELA

It binds the threads of fate with gentle hand,

# ANGELA

A bond unbroken, strong enough to stand.

# ANGELA

So let us raise our voices high and clear,

# ANGELA

In praise of Angela, ever dear.

# ANGELA

Her name, a beacon in the darkest night,

# ANGELA

A guiding star, forever burning bright.

# ANGELA

In the realm of dreams where fantasies unfurl,

# ANGELA

Angela's name, a vision to behold.

# ANGELA

It paints the canvas of the sleeping mind,

# ANGELA

A muse divine, forever intertwined.

# ANGELA

# ABOUT THE AUTHOR

Walter the Educator is one of the pseudonyms for Walter Anderson. Formally educated in Chemistry, Business, and Education, he is an educator, an author, a diverse entrepreneur, and he is the son of a disabled war veteran. "Walter the Educator" shares his time between educating and creating. He holds interests and owns several creative projects that entertain, enlighten, enhance, and educate, hoping to inspire and motivate you.

Follow, find new works, and stay up to date
with Walter the Educator™
at WaltertheEducator.com

www.ingramcontent.com/pod-product-compliance
Lightning Source LLC
LaVergne TN
LVHW052009060526
838201LV00059B/3937